RELEVANCE
The Role of Christianity
in the
Twentieth Century

RELEVANCE

The Role of Christianity
in the Twentieth Century

by
Richard C. Halverson

Word Books, Publishers
Waco, Texas—London England

First Printing—August 1968
Second Printing—March 1969

Grateful acknowledgment is made for permission to use the
following quotations: selections from *The Revised Standard
Version of the Bible,* copyright © 1946, 1952 by the Division of
Christian Education of the National Council of Churches in the
United States of America; a quotation from *Encounter with
Spurgeon,* copyright 1963 by Fortress Press (Philadelphia);
and lines from the Introduction to *Letters to Young Churches*
by J. B. Phillips, copyright 1947 by The Macmillan Company
(New York).

Library of Congress Catalog Number: 68-31111
Printed in the United States of America

To
The Session
of the Fourth Presbyterian Church
whose
friendship, encouragement,
fatherly and brotherly guidance
have been
one of life's richest benefits

PREFACE

Was Jesus relevant?

His contemporary world took little notice of Him. He didn't make the headlines. He had somewhat of a reputation as an itinerant teacher and "miracle worker," but the sophisticated Romans and Greeks did not take Him seriously. Although He attracted the attention of thousands during His brief public ministry, He was alone at the end. He had no advocate at the trial. No effort was made to stay His execution. Except for a pitiful band of disorganized, disillusioned disciples, Jesus exited as He had entered— unnoticed either by the civil authorities or the general public.

Was Jesus relevant? In the context of His own time, that is?

Apparently His contemporaries did not think so . . . They crucified Him!

President John F. Kennedy had just addressed the nation on television with reference to his confrontation with Soviet Russia in Cuba. In response to an invitation, I flew to Billings, Montana, for a conference. At the airport a very close friend, a strong admirer of the President, greeted me. After the amenities, I said, "How would you like to be in the White House right now?" Quizzically he responded, "What do you mean?"

"How would you like to be in Kennedy's shoes, with his responsibility for decisive action in Cuba?"

He was thoughtful for a moment, then, "I'd like to be in the White House now. That's where history is being made!"

His answer surprised me, and I couldn't get it out of my mind as we drove to the conference. Finally, I said, "Willis, how many political leaders of the first century can you remember? How many Caesars or Roman senators or Greek city fathers?" His silence was his answer.

"Who do we remember from that first century besides Jesus?"

Slowly he repeated, "Paul . .. Peter . . . Andrew . . . John . . . Thomas . . . Barnabas . . . James . . . Philip . . . Matthew . . ."

The fact is, these unlettered, unknown, unsophisticated, and in at least one instance, disreputable men were making the most significant history of their day. They were of little moment to the power elite, and if "relevance" were of any concern to the culture of their day, they certainly would have been rated of insignificant status.

Yet never has a teacher, never have disciples, never has a movement been more relevant!

CONTENTS

HOW IS THE GOSPEL RELEVANT?

How is love relevant to loneliness?
   Hope to despair?
      Direction to drift?
         Purpose to meaninglessness?
            Fulfillment to frustration?
               How is food relevant to hunger?

Water to thirst?
   Light to darkness?
      Rest to exhaustion?
         Life to death?
            Resurrection to the grave?

Ironically, those whose slogan is relevance may be the ones who most risk being swept along passively and blindly by the march of time. It sometimes seems as though they would preserve Christianity in the world by baptizing as 'Christian' whatever they find thriving in the world: psychotherapy . . . urban renewal . . . sexual revolution . . . and finally, atheism.

. . . there is grave risk that the seeming 'relevance' of special ventures, such as direct social action, may be an evasion of the responsibility to respond to God in one's own station and to set right the affairs of one's own life.

(From Princeton Seminary Bulletin, June 1967, by James E. Dittes, Faculty of Yale Divinity School, entitled, *The Relevance of Being Irrelevant.*)

ILLUSION IN RELEVANCE

Then said Jesus, Father, forgive them; for they know not what they do. And they parted his raiment, and cast lots.

And the people stood beholding. And the rulers also with them derided him, saying, He saved others; let him save himself, if he be Christ, the chosen of God.

And the soldiers also mocked him, coming to him, and offering him vinegar,

And saying, If thou be the king of the Jews, save thyself.

And a superscription also was written over him in letters of Greek, and Latin, and Hebrew, THIS IS THE KING OF THE JEWS.

And one of the malefactors which were hanged railed on him, saying, If thou be Christ, save thyself and us.

Luke 23: 34-39

Chapter 1

ILLUSION IN RELEVANCE

Relevance is a key word in contemporary vernacular. It has been over-used and misused. For many it has become merely a glib cliché, carelessly and thoughtlessly sprinkled, for effect, throughout sterile cocktail hour patter. But, for the person in serious quest of spiritual truth, *relevance* is an intensely significant and colorful word that insists upon close scrutiny. However, as a backdrop to our consideration, I want to ask several provocative questions, which, hopefully, will result in satisfactory answers as we search together for an authentic meaning of relevance on the pages to follow.

According to the New Testament, Jesus gave sight to three blind men, made the deaf to hear, the dumb to speak, the crippled to walk. He healed lepers, and in three instances, restored life to the dead. On two occasions He fed huge crowds with a few scraps of food. In short, He did a great deal to alleviate human suffering and wretchedness in the three short years of His ministry. Unquestionably, Jesus launched a forceful and effective assault on disease, poverty, famine, and death—those universal enemies of mankind.

Did He do this for all who were stricken? Did He heal everyone who was sick, give speech to all who were dumb, or hearing to all who were deaf? Were all of the lepers and cripples healed? Did He feed everyone who was hungry and raise all who were dead? We know that He didn't—but, why not? If He could do this for some, why not more? Why not all? If He could touch blind eyes and make them see, why would he leave anyone blind? If He could take a few loaves and fishes and feed fifteen to twenty thousand people, why should anyone go hungry? Was He unaware that there were others who were blind and deaf and dumb and leprous and hungry? Hardly. If He was aware of this need all about Him, was He indifferent to it? No, we cannot believe this about the man who was the very prototype of human compassion and love. Had He reached the limit of His ability to do these things? Had He run out of power? This is hardly reasonable.

As a matter of fact, why did He permit Himself to be crucified? He stated clearly that "No man takes My life from Me, I lay it down of Myself, I take it up again. I have the power to lay it down. I have the power to take it up again." When Jesus stood before Pilate, Pilate was aggravated by His silence, and under the pressure of that decisive moment commanded, "Speak to me, don't you know I have the power to crucify you, the power to release you?" Jesus responded by saying, "You have no power over Me at all, except it be given you from above."

The Jewish leaders had plotted His arrest many times

during the course of His three year ministry, always without success. But when Jesus was finally apprehended in the garden, He voluntarily submitted to the armed mob. He had said to His disciples, "My time is at hand." The last word He cried on the cross was "Finished!" as though what He had come to do was accomplished, and then the record says, "He gave up the ghost." He died on the cross, voluntarily. He literally laid down His life by sheer volition.

If Jesus Christ had such remarkable, final control of His destiny, why did He not refuse crucifixion, remain alive, and devote Himself to the elimination of all human wretchedness and tragedy? Why didn't He, if He could? He demonstrated He could, then why? Why did He submit to crucifixion? This question, you see, is really implicit in the mockery that taunted Him on the cross. He was challenged three times to save Himself: The rulers, "If He be Christ, let Him save Himself"; the soldiers, "If you are the King of the Jews, save yourself"; and the thief, "If you are Christ, save yourself and us."

To answer intelligently these and other related questions we must clarify the meaning and intent of the word *relevance*. It can be very misleading, and therein lies the illusion, the deception, the peril. Some definition is fundamental to our responsibility as Christians in this contemporary world which is demanding relevance. What is relevance? Is it a pragmatic test—something that works? Even more personally, does it work for me? Does it work in my situation? Does it address itself to the real problem? Does it give answers that are valid? Actually, the word, relevance, cannot stand in isolation, because it involves relationship. It means to be related, to be appropriate, to be germane, to be suitable. It is a relative term and therefore can be understood only in application to objects, or things, or people, or circumstances. In other words, when one asks, "Is the Christian faith relevant?" it is quite proper to reply, "Relevant to what?"

It is precisely in the context of relevance that Christian faith is being tested today, and not uncommonly, on the basis of inverted values, it is being repudiated. In the name of relevance men are insisting that Christianity serve one human system or another; and if it does not work for whatever system championed, it is presumed irrelevant and invalid. There are some who insist that Christianity must be socialistic or capitalistic—Christianity must be liberal (economically, politically and socially, that is) or conservative. They insist that Christianity must serve segregation or integration, democracy or totalitarianism. By such false criteria Christians are being divided. For example, recently I slipped and said "sinners and republicans," instead of "sinners and publicans"—everyone present laughed. But there may an insidious implication behind such laughter. I have met Republicans who honestly believe a Democrat cannot be a Christian, and I have met Democrats who feel the same way about Republicans.

There are people who insist that it is impossible to be a Christian and be a political, economic, or social liberal. Others are equally insistent that a person cannot be a Christian and be an economic, political, or social conservative. How absurd! But, many persons today are actually locking the gospel of Jesus Christ to human systems and demanding relevance on their limited terms. If Christianity does not produce, it is rejected—as Jesus Christ was rejected when He hung on the cross.

[18]

Again, the issue was clearly drawn in the challenge of the thief, "If Thou be Christ, save Thyself and us." Such was the contempt of this criminal for the dying Savior! But Jesus has been indicted with that same challenge in every successive generation—even by many who claimed to be His friends. Actually, the thief had a false idea of Christ's purpose. "If Thou be Christ, save us." As far as he was concerned, the integrity of Jesus Christ rested on his own personal, immediate physical relief. "Get me out of this mess or you are not Jesus Christ." He was saying, in effect, prove that you are the Messiah by getting me off this cross and out from under the penalty of my life of crime. The condemned thief stipulated the conditions under which he would take Jesus Christ seriously—"You conform to my demands, and I will go along with you."

Indeed, by his superficial thinking and myopic reasoning, that thief has many modern disciples—persons who assert the conditions under which they will honor God! As far as they are concerned, like the thief, Christ is to be judged according to their own personal interpretation of relevance—and if Christ is going to be acceptable, He must conform to their standards. Characteristic of such interpretations and standards is that the criteria for relevance is always worldly (I didn't say materialistic), always this-worldly, always this side of the grave, always physical. In whatever pious context it is put, Christ is judged on commercial grounds—in terms of self-interest. To interpret the relevance of Jesus Christ in terms of our prejudice and self-interest is a ludicrous perversion, whether that prejudice would drive a person to leave his church in anger because of Negro worshipers or to ride some pet theological hobby to an obnoxious conclusion. And the

[19]

incredible fact is that there are those in the church today who are so utterly consumed by the passion to fit God into their twisted notions of purpose and relevance that those on the "outside" cannot help but misread the gospel. How prone we are to say, with the thief on the cross, "If you are Christ save us!" Save us physically. Save us with our prejudice. Preserve *our* ideas and interpretations. But in so doing we fail completely to understand Christ's purpose in history.

The thief also had a false idea of the Messiah. He was not only completely wrong as to the purpose for which Jesus had entered history; he failed to comprehend the means whereby this purpose was to be achieved. He said, "If Thou be Christ save Thyself." One never ceases to be amazed at the stubborn and perennial conspiracy to eliminate the crucifixion from Christian faith. It must be masterminded by some transcendent force. Even Peter tried. This particular event occurred just after that revealing witness and confession of Peter in which he boldly proclaimed that Jesus was "the Christ, the Son of the living God." Jesus was attempting to prepare His disciples for His coming rendezvous with death in Jerusalem in which He would "suffer many things from the elders and chief priests and scribes, and be killed, and on the third day be raised." At this very moment we read that Peter "began to rebuke him, saying, 'God forbid, Lord! This shall never happen to you.' "

A further attempt to cancel out the crucifixion came indirectly through Jewish leadership when they taunted Him with the idea that He could prove that He was really the Son of God by coming down from the cross: "He saved others; he cannot save himself. He is the King of Israel;

[20]

let him come down now from the cross, and we will believe in him." And following the crucifixion we read the account of the two disciples traveling the dusty road to Emmaus. They were wretched and despondent—thoroughly convinced that Jesus' death was a tragic mistake. Their hopes were crushed in what they believed to be the complete frustration of His historical purpose.

This recurring effort on the part of humanity to remove the cross of Christ from Christian faith, is monotonous by its regularity and its consistency.

Jesus Christ's purpose in history transcended all the ideas and systems and utopias of men. It was an eternal purpose, only in terms of which history has any meaning; and this purpose required that He willingly sacrifice His life on the cross.

Read carefully this remarkable statement made by Mario Savio, the young leader of the free speech movement on the campus of the University of California at Berkeley. Savio was addressing the Trotskyites Young Socialist Alliance, explaining the student protest to them. He said: "The most important concept for understanding the student movement is Marx's notion of alienation. Its basic meaning is that the worker is alienated from his product, but the concept is applicable to students too. Students are frustrated. They can find no place in society where alienation doesn't exist, where they can do meaningful work. Despair sets in, a volatile political agent. The students revolt against the apparatus of the university. This is the motive power of the student movement!" Amazing! A brilliant, vocal, militant student leader diagnoses the root problem as alienation and meaninglessness, or purposelessness. It is almost as if he is drawing from Scripture.

[21]

Why did Jesus Christ enter history and lay down His life on the cross? Because men were alienated from God, therefore from each other, and life had no meaning; they were lost! Jesus' purpose was to reconcile men to God so they would no longer be aliens from God and each other. Isn't it interesting that the heart and core of the Christian faith addresses itself precisely to the problem that this student leader spoke about at the University of California? This is relevance!

Now back to the question. Why did Jesus Christ not remain alive and eliminate, generation by generation, all the evils which harass humanity? Simply because He was the Great Physician, and in the finest tradition of medical science, He was unwilling to remain preoccupied with the symptoms when He could destroy the disease. Jesus Christ was unwilling to settle for anything less than elimination of the cause of all evil in history.

The picture is ludicrous, but I want to give it to you because it is analagous. Suppose years ago that medical science had decided we were wasting our time and our money and our energy on research. For example, rather than waste time and funds researching poliomylitis, we can use that money to mass produce iron lungs. Then when people get polio we will have a lung available, free. Can you conceive, off somewhere in the future, of a civilization sustained by iron lungs! Millions of people who had contracted this disease, are kept alive by an iron lung.

This is precisely what our modern world is asking Christianity to do in principle. Jesus Christ knew that poverty, prejudice, human wretchedness, illness, tragedy, war and death, were due to a malignancy in the human heart which could be cured only by His own sacrifice on the cross. He entered history and determined a course that ultimately took him to the cross to solve this root problem, once and for all—forever.

"I am not ashamed of the gospel of Christ for it is the power of God unto salvation to everyone that believes, the Jew first, and also to the Greek." That is relevance! "The blood of Jesus Christ, God's son, cleanses from all sin." That is relevance!

A SIMPLE STATEMENT OF FACT

Because that, when they knew God, they glorified him not as God, neither were thankful; but became vain in their imaginations, and their foolish heart was darkened.

Wherefore God also gave them up to uncleanness through the lusts of their own hearts, to dishonor their own bodies between themselves:

Who changed the truth of God into a lie, and worshiped and served the creature more than the Creator, who is blessed for ever. Amen.

For this cause God gave them up unto vile affections for even their women did change the natural use into that which is against nature:

And likewise also the men, leaving the natural use of the woman, burned in their lust one toward another; men with men working that which is unseemly, and receiving in themselves that recompense of their error which was meet.

And even as they did not like to retain God in their knowledge, God gave them over to a reprobate mind, to do those things which are not convenient;

Being filled with all unrighteousness, fornication, wickedness, covetousness, maliciousness; full of envy, murder, debate, deceit, malignity; whisperers,

Backbiters, haters of God, despiteful, proud, boasters, inventors of evil things, disobedient to parents,

Without understanding, covenant breakers, without natural affection, implacable, unmerciful:

Who knowing the judgment of God, that they which commit such things are worthy of death, not only do the same, but have pleasure in them that do them.

Romans 1:21, 24-32

Chapter 2

A SIMPLE STATEMENT OF FACT

"Righteousness exalteth a nation: but sin is a reproach to any people." The relevance of these words for our times is indisputable. It is an incontestable fact that our moral and spiritual structures are severely threatened and seem to be crumbling. We have been invaded by a restlessness, an uneasiness—a throbbing awareness that "all is not right with the world." For this reason, it seems to me that this profound comment from Proverbs is due a close look, and if rightly understood and applied it will make a dynamic impact on our country and the world.

These words are not a threat, not even a warning. They are simply a statement of fact. It is like saying, "The shortest distance between two points is a straight line." It is like saying, "Water equals two parts hydrogen, one part oxygen." It is like saying, "Fire burns, cold freezes." Actually, this is a simple statement of principle, a law of life which is inherent in the universe, in the world, in human nature, in history. These remarkable words assert the simple fact that spiritual and moral health is constructive and beneficial; that spiritual and moral sickness is destructive. This is without controversy. The decline and fall of every great social, political, economic order and/or system in history is clear confirmation of this truth. This basic principle is working every day in the life of every person in the world. It is operative every day in our home and family life, in all the structures of society, in every area of life. Its process is inexorable, despite every effort of sophisticated man to rationalize and disregard it. The results of righteous living bless any nation. The degeneration, disintegration, and demise of any and all people is inevitable if sinful practices are followed. This is a simple fact of life—it is just the way things are.

Now, let's take a closer look at the negative phrase, "Sin is a reproach to any people"—the inevitable destructiveness of sin. The Apostle Paul made some pretty plain and blunt statements in the first chapter of Romans. Reread this chapter and notice the vicious, downward spiral—the awful abyss into which humanity inescapably sinks through sin. A description of the descent begins at the 21st verse: "Because that when they knew God, they glorified him not as God, neither were thankful . . ." This is the root of sin: failure or refusal to worship God. This is secularism, the spirit opposed to faith in God. Actually, a contemporary wording of our verse could well be, "Godliness exalteth a nation; secularism is a reproach to any people." Then, because of their failure to be thankful to God they became "vain in their imaginations, and their foolish heart was darkened. Professing themselves to be wise, they became fools." Intellectual and emotional degeneration

[28]

are inevitable when men refuse God! Next comes spiritual
degeneration (Rom. 1:23). These wise fools whose intel-
lects were darkened because they would not acknowledge
God, "Changed the glory of the uncorruptible God into an
image made like to corruptible man, and to birds, and
four-footed beasts, and creeping things." Social degeneration follows (Rom. 1:24), "Wherefore God also gave
them up." A whole humanity—God gave up "to uncleanness through the lusts of their own hearts, to dishonor their
own bodies between themselves." The ineluctable process
continues (verse 25); they "changed the truth of God
into a lie." (Here is a 180 degree spiritual and moral inver-
sion: black is white, error is truth, chaos is order.) They
"changed the truth of God into a lie and worshiped and
served the creature more than the Creator." Now, note
the terrible consequences, the perversion of personality—
(verses 26-27), "For this cause God gave them up unto
vile affection, for even their women did change the natural
use into that which is against nature; likewise also the men,
leaving the natural use of the woman, burned in their lust
one toward another; men with men, working that which is
unseemly and receiving in themselves [that is receiving
in their own personalities] that recompense of their error
which was meet."

Finally, beginning at verse 28, complete degeneration:
"Even as they did not like to retain God in their knowledge God gave them over to a reprobate mind." There is
no power on earth to stop the human mind from becoming
wicked if God is rejected. The mind that will not worship
God becomes corrupt. This is inescapable, as inescapable
as fire's burning. "God gave them over to a reprobate mind
to do those things which are not convenient." Now we see

[29]

total breakdown. "Being filled with all unrighteousness, fornication, wickedness, covetousness, maliciousness, full of envy, murder, debate, deceit, malignity; whisperers, Backbiters, haters of God, despiteful, proud, boasters, inventors of evil things, disobedient to parents, Without understanding, covenant breakers (contract breakers), without natural affection, implacable, unmerciful." Then in verse 32, we see the very ultimate in human degradation, "Who knowing the judgment of God, that they which commit such things are worthy of death, not only do the same, but have pleasure in them that do them." They want to see it on the screen, on the stage; they want to read it in books; they want it in advertising. It is not enough to do it; they want to see it done; they take pleasure in it; they are entertained by it. There is nowhere else to go! This is the dead end. This build-up of degeneration in human personality, collectively and individually, winds up (or down) to the ultimate in depravity—vicarious enjoyment of lust, depravity, sin.

But this is ancient literature, written nineteen hundred years ago! What of our contemporary world? *Time* magazine, March 5, 1965, reports that progressive church thinkers now state that "the twentieth century sexual revolution directly challenges Christianity's teachings, Biblical teaching against fornication and adultery. As an alternative they propose an ethic based on love rather than law, in which the ultimate criterion for right and wrong is not Divine command but the individual's subjective perception of what is good for himself and his neighbor in each given situation." In other words, I am my own law! I decide what is right for me. You decide what is right for you. *Time* continues: "Church leaders are quoted as saying that no sexual relationship should be absolutely condemned by the Church." And then Joseph Fletcher of the Episcopal Theological School is quoted as saying: "One enters into every decision-making moment armed with the wisdom of the culture," (the wisdom of a Godless therefore reprobate mind) "but prepared in one's freedom to suspend and violate any rule, except one must as responsibly as possible seek the good of one's neighbor."

The truth about atheistic existentialism is now clear. This mysterious word is beginning to make sense now that the fruit of its teaching is beginning to mature. Amazing, isn't it, that some intellectuals brand these teachings and conclusions as modern! Isaiah wrote seven hundred years before Christ—twenty-six hundred years ago, "All we like sheep have gone astray, we have turned everyone to his own way." Isaiah did not call it "situational ethics," he called it sin. Again, in Proverbs 12:15 and 21:2: "The way of the fool is right in his own eyes," and "Every way of a man is right in his own eyes." The labels may be new, but the idea is old! Call it what you will, it is spiritual and moral anarchy.

Although I believe in the principle of human rights and am personally convinced of the rightness of the present movement, I cannot help but comment in this context on the glaring one-sided promotion of so-called civil rights, which one leader has defined as a "blank check payable on demand." Why do we not hear something about civic responsibility. Rights without responsibility do not add up to freedom; this leads ultimately to chaos and bondage. However evil has been the exploitation of the past, irresponsibility is not a solution. Two wrongs do not add up to a right.

[31]

The point of the Scripture text is indisputable: sin leads to individual and collective ruin. Sin guarantees the breakdown of all human social systems, and there is only one solution: "Righteousness exalteth a nation."

The word "righteousness" in both Hebrew and Greek is a simple word. In this day when much dialogue is nothing more than semantic duel, people are rationalizing the meaning of words. This is part of the perversion that is inherent in a godless culture. But the word is clear in Hebrew and in Greek. It means "rightness, justice, virtue." It means to be chaste. It is implied in words such as quality, integrity, honesty, responsibility. To be righteous is to be right with God and right with your neighbor. Righteousness includes purity in motive as well as propriety in method. It means reverence for God and concern for others. It means fair play, truthfulness, unselfishness, humility, kindness, charity. Righteousness means Christ-likeness.

Unquestionably, we have been looking at a rather dismal scene, but, thank God, there can be another chapter. And that chapter can be written by you and me—that is, if we are willing to pay the price for authentic relevance. But, if we go about our daily affairs absolving ourselves of responsibility, we actually become a part of the problem that is ravaging our nation and our world. The solution begins with us as persons. Each of us in his own way can become instruments in the hands of God for reconciliation. If we have the determination to be Christ-managed, we will become an influence for righteousness right where we are. If we have the courage to speak when we are intimidated to silence, and if we are willing to be silent when we ought not to speak, God will lead us by His grace, through His Spirit.

Therefore, let us determine together to do three things: First, to repent of our sin, our fears, our willingness to let this mess go on and on and on, without even speaking against it—to repent of our lack of moral indignation. Second, let us give ourselves totally to Jesus Christ as instruments of righteousness right where we are. Let Him be the motivating force, the dominating influence in every area of life—home, business, social, and political. Third, whatever He tells us to do, obey without question or concern for consequences. Let us dare to obey Christ, even if the whole world is against us!

REASONABLE FEAR

The disciple is not above his master, nor the servant above his lord.

It is enough for the disciple that he be as his master, and the servant as his lord. If they have called the master of the house Beelzebub, how much more shall they call them of his household?

Fear them not therefore: for there is nothing covered, that shall not be revealed; and hid, that shall not be known.

What I tell you in darkness, that speak ye in light: and what ye hear in the ear, that preach ye upon the housetops.

And fear not them which kill the body, but are not able to kill the soul: but rather fear him which is able to destroy both soul and body in hell.

Matthew 10: 24-28

Chapter 3

REASONABLE FEAR

There are fears which are irrational, unnecessary, illusory, unfounded. Jesus spoke out against fear—"Fear not, little flock"—"Let not your heart be troubled." But there is a fear that is rational, real, redemptive. Fear is a valid motive. We teach a child to fear fire. We instruct a little girl to fear the man who attempts to pick her up in his car when she is walking home from school. The wise parent and counselor makes certain that the consequences of certain destructive practices are clearly understood. Fear is fundamental to education; fear is fundamental to life. Russell Kirk in a Chicago address based upon the text, "The fear of the Lord is the beginning of wisdom," said, "Without knowledge of fear we cannot know order in personality or society. Fear is an ineluctable part of the human condition. If fear is lacking, hope and aspirations fail. To demand from mankind freedom from fear as politically attainable was a silly piece of demagogic sophistry.

If fear were wiped out altogether from our lives, we would be desperately bored, longing for old or new terrors. There are things which rightfully we ought to fear if we are to enjoy our dignity as men. To fear to commit evil, to hate what is abominable, is the mark of manliness."

Then he quotes a striking passage from Shaw's book, *Back to Methuselah:* "Good-natured, unambitious men are cowards when they have no religion. At the spectacle of half of Europe being kicked to death by the other half they stare in helpless horror, or are persuaded by the newspapers that this is a sound commercial investment and an act of Divine justice. They [good-natured, unambitious men without religion] are dominated and exploited, not only by greedy and often half-witted and half-alive weaklings who will do anything for cigars, champagne, motor cars, and the more childish and selfish uses of money, but by able and sound administrators who can do nothing else with them than dominate and exploit them. Government and exploitation become synonymous under such circumstances, and the world is finally ruled by the childish, the brigands and the blackguards."

Kirk continues: "Freedom from fear, if I read St. John right, is one of the planks in the platform of the anti-Christ. Such freedom is purchased only at the cost of spiritual and political enslavement. It ends at Armageddon. Lacking conviction that 'the fear of the Lord is the beginning of wisdom,' the captains and kings yield to the fierce ideologues, the merciless adventurers, the charlatans, and the metaphysically mad, and then truly when the stern, righteous God of fear and love has been denied, the savage God lays down his new commandments. Yes, from the post-Christian church [Kirk is referring to the

[38]

contemporary church] the dusty fear of God and the odor of sanctity have been quite cleansed. Within the doors there remains, spiritually speaking, simply a vacuum which nature abhors. Presently, something will fill that vacuum, perhaps a rough beast, its hour come round at last, with a stench of death in its fur." *Men who fear God face life fearlessly. Men who do not fear God end up fearing everything.*

Jesus said that we are to fear. Whom are we to fear? What are we to fear? He said, "Fear not them which kill the body, but are not able to kill the soul: but rather fear him which is able to destroy both soul and body in hell." This admonition was spoken in the context of persecution. "Behold," Jesus said to His disciples, "I send you forth as sheep in the midst of wolves. They will deliver you up to the councils and they will scourge you in the synagogues, and ye shall be hated of all men for My name's sake"; but, said Jesus, do not fear them. Do not be afraid of them! "Fear not them that can destroy the body, but not the soul."

Does this mean that Jesus was indifferent to the physical welfare of men? Does this mean that the Church is to be indifferent to the physical welfare of men? The answer is obvious. The question is almost sacrilegious, and its answer is superfluous. Who cared more or did more for men's bodies? Wherever the Church has gone with the gospel of Christ she has brought enlightenment, compassion, and healing. The Church has led in giving the world schools and colleges, progressive agricultural methods, hospitals, clinics, orphanages, widows' homes, and care for the aging. Like rivers of compassion the mission of the Church has flowed into valleys of need around the world. Centuries before anybody ever thought of foreign aid or a Peace Corps the Church was there meeting and ministering to the bodies and minds of men, and she continues her work throughout the world to this very moment. Jesus was not indifferent to physical suffering, nor is His Church. The church that is faithful to the gospel does not ignore the physical sufferings of men.

But Jesus did teach that the antidote to irrational and unnecessary fear is a greater fear, a basic fear. Who is to be feared? What is to be feared? Now at this point scholarship is divided on the text. Some say the "him" in the verse, "Fear him who is able to destroy both soul and body in hell," refers to the devil, on the grounds that the verses following, 29 through 31, in which Jesus speaks of the loving concern of the Father, would be out of place if God were the One to be feared. Others argue that it is God who is to be feared: "The fear of the Lord is the beginning of wisdom." I am inclined to believe that the reference is to fear God Who is able to destroy both soul and body in hell.At any rate, the one to be feared may not be absolutely clear in the text, but there is no doubt at all as to *what* is to be feared: the destruction of the soul and body in hell. Jesus is saying, according to one commentator, "Fear not the persecutor but the tempter. Don't be afraid of the man who kills you for your fidelity, but fear the man who wants to buy you off, and the devil whose agent he is." Jesus is arguing for the incalculable value of one man's soul. "What shall it profit a man if he gain the whole world and lose his own soul?" Of what lasting value is it to feed and clothe a person and completely neglect his spiritual needs and his future destiny?

Note these direct and pointed comments and warnings—

they are relevant. Jesus said, "So shall it be at the end
of the world: the angels shall come forth, and sever the
wicked from among the just, And shall cast them into
the furnace of fire (that is, Gehenna, the word Hell, not
Hades, which Jesus used here): and there shall be wailing
and gnashing of teeth" (Matt. 13:49, 50). Jesus said,
"Then shall he say also unto them on the left hand, De-
part from me, ye cursed, into everlasting fire prepared for
the devil and his angels" (Matt. 25:41). Again, "It is
better for thee to enter into life maimed, than having two
hands to go into hell, into the fire, that never shall be
quenched" (Mark 9:43). In the book of Revelation we
read, "The same shall drink of the wine of the wrath of
God, which is poured out without mixture into the cup
of his indignation; and he shall be tormented with fire
and brimstone" (Rev. 14:10). "The devil that deceived
them was cast into the lake of fire and brimstone, where
the beast and the false prophet are, and shall be tormented
day and night forever and ever . . . And whosoever was
not found written in the book of life was cast into this
lake of fire" (Rev. 20:10,15). Now, we are perfectly
free to ignore or reject these Biblical teachings and warnings as ancient superstition. We may believe this is a lot
of nonsense, but I earnestly recommend that, as intelligent
discipline, these words be thoughtfully considered before
they are laid aside lightly and ignored.

Can you think of any leader you would trust more than
one who was motivated by a healthy fear, or reverence,
of Almighty God and the eternally destructive power of
evil? Or can you think of anything worse than a church or
a Christian, warned and informed of the destiny of the
lost, that would ignore the salvation of men's souls in its

preoccupation with sociological, economic, and political concern? In the Church, the gospel is always relevant to life as we find it here and now.

In the matter of mission, the Church of Jesus Christ is absolutely unique in history. She exists for the salvation of men. No other organization or institution has this mission. There are hundreds of organizations, in addition to government itself, which exist for the social welfare of men; and, incidentally, these organizations are manned in great part by church people and receive a great part of their financial support from church people. And they are doing what they are designed to do. But, their purpose is not directed to the eternal spiritual welfare of men. If the Church fails here, there is no organization that will fill the breach. The Church cannot, must not, default in this mission, however busy she may be in her care and concern for men.

Humanitarianism is not Christianity. The central purpose of the Church and of every individual Christian is to witness to the Lordship of Jesus Christ as the Savior of everyone who will accept Him as the Lord of life in this world and in the world to come—beyond the grave. This is relevance.

MISSION—RECONCILIATION

For the love of Christ constraineth us; because we thus judge, that if one died for all, then were all dead:

And that he died for all, that they which live should not henceforth live unto themselves, but unto him which died for them, and rose again.

Wherefore henceforth know we no man after the flesh: yea, though we have known Christ after the flesh, yet now henceforth know we him no more.

Therefore if any man be in Christ, he is a new creature: old things are passed away; behold, all things are become new.

And all things are of God, who hath reconciled us to himself by Jesus Christ, and hath given to us the ministry of reconciliation;

To wit, that God was in Christ, reconciling the world unto himself, not imputing their trespasses unto them; and hath committed unto us the word of reconciliation.

Now then we are ambassadors for Christ, as though God did beeseech you by us: we pray you in Christ's stead, be ye reconciled to God.

For he hath made him to be sin for us, who knew no sin; that we might be made the righteousness of God in him.
                                          2 Corinthians 5:14-21

Chapter 4

MISSION—RECONCILIATION

Should we attempt to reduce to one word a description of history and of our contemporary dilemma, we could not find a better word than "rift." We live in a fragmented world—a broken world, internationally. There are two great power blocks locked in mortal conflict, grinding between them many small nations who are struggling for neutrality and independence. There are two Germanys, two Koreas, two Chinas, two Viet Nams.

Racially—we are very conscious of the rift between the black and white in America, but in one way or another every nation suffers this rift between its peoples. Economically—there are the desperately poor and the exorbitantly rich and affluent, the haves and the have nots. Intellectually—multiplied millions remain illiterate coincident with an unprecedented explosion of knowledge. Industrially—the labor-management rift, still a problem in America, is fast emerging in other nations of the world.

Domestically—we see the disintegration of the home through alienation between parents and children, between husbands and wives. And perhaps worst of all, there is the rift within man himself—fragmented personalities, a devastating civil war within men producing anxieties and fears, neuroses and psychoses. Even the Church is fragmented, and today, as rarely in history, she suffers relentless tension.

Here is a problem of relevance. What is the answer to this broken world? Where is healing for this earth rent by schism? The Bible answer, the intelligent answer, the one adequate answer, can be summed up in a word, "reconciliation." The Bible reveals that the fundamental rift in history, producing all other divisions, is alienation between man and God. Man voluntarily alienated from God is disoriented in the world God created to be his home. Lost and disoriented, man is out of gear with God's order, therefore, he does not mesh with his fellowmen individually or in a group. To bridge this tragic rift, God has spoken in the Person of His Son, Jesus Christ—"God was in Christ, reconciling the world to Himself." Paul says in another place, "For he has made known to us in all wisdom and insight the mystery of his will, according to his purpose which he set forth in Christ as a plan for the fullness of time, to unite all things in him" (Ephesians 1:9-10 RSV). And, "Through him to reconcile to himself all things, making peace by the blood of his cross" (Colossians 1:20 RSV).

Paul's statement in 2 Corinthians 5:15-21 sums up thoroughly the mission of Jesus Christ in the world and the mandate He gave His Church. All Christian responsibility and mission begin here. This is basic to the relevance

[46]

of the Church to the world. Christians are to be agents of reconciliation. Paul says, "All things are of God, who hath reconciled us to himself by Jesus Christ, and hath given to us the ministry of reconciliation; To wit, that God was in Christ, reconciling the world to himself, not imputing their trespasses unto them; and hath committed unto us the word of reconciliation." "God has given to us the ministry of reconciliation." "God has committed to us the word of reconciliation."

The ministry of reconciliation, the word of reconciliation, are our inescapable mandate. Our lives, individually and collectively, must square with this commission if we are to be truly Christian. To make it very personal, do you have a disruptive influence where you are, or do you bring peace? Do you bring division, or do you unite? Do you alienate men, or do you reconcile? Does your life have a unifying, reconciling, uniting influence, or does it have an alienating, disruptive, dis-peaceful influence? Do you bring peace, or do you bring strife as a person?

What is the word of reconciliation? This is essential to the understanding of these words. Unfortunately, this passage has been one of the most misused and abused in the Bible. In the name of relevance men have used these words to justify programs designed only to reconcile man with man, while at the same time ignoring evangelism and the explicit purpose of reconciling man to God. Again and again, we hear this passage referred to as grounds for purely humanitarian or sociological movements in the name of relevance, thereby rendering it utterly irrelevant. The reconciliation referred to here does not stop with individual redemption or salvation, but it begins there. All Christian sociology and ethics begin with man's rightness with God through Jesus Christ, according to Paul. If men are to be reconciled to each other ultimately, they first must be reconciled to God individually. Individual salvation which does not issue in authentic social responsibility is sub-Christian.

This is the word of reconciliation: Christ died, Christ rose. Paul says, "We thus judge if one died for all, then we are all dead, and that he died for all that they which live should not henceforth live unto themselves, but unto him which died and rose again." Note the context of this passage. Paul begins the chapter (2 Corinthians 5) with a gracious, thrilling prospect beyond the grave: "Whilst we are at home in the body, we are absent from the Lord." Then he discusses the very passion of his own life: "To be accepted of the Lord." He speaks of the certainty of judgment. He speaks of "the terror of the Lord," which he says compels him to persuade men to be reconciled to God. This is the word of reconciliation.

Paul continues, "Therefore if any man be in Christ, he is a new creature: old things are passed away; behold, all things are become new." This is the word of reconciliation, the promise of a changed human nature, power that can transform human nature from selfishness to selflessness; from self-seeking to self-sacrificing. This cannot be done by social structures. They have been tried, but they break down because of the stubborn fact of pride or selfishness in the human heart. As one man put it, "No matter how cleverly you organize bad eggs, you can't get a good omelet."

Paul, constrained by God to go to Corinth—the wickedest city in one of the most depraved cultures in history— faced the deplorable social and moral conditions there with these words: "When I came to you brethren I came not with excellency of speech or of wisdom, declaring unto you the testimony of God, for I determined not to know anything among you save Jesus Christ, and him crucified." So far as this brilliant Jew was concerned, relevance to Corinth meant Christ crucified. Why? Jesus had said, "There is nothing from without a man, that entering into him can defile him! But the things which come out of him, those are they that defile the man." And then He added, when His disciples asked Him to amplify, that everything which defiles human nature has its origin inside the human heart. It isn't how you organize human nature; it is something inside of human nature that is the problem. In an address which Albert Einstein made in 1948 he said, "I do not fear the explosive power of the atom bomb. What I fear is the explosive power of evil in the human heart." What is the answer to the explosive power of evil in the human heart? Where is the answer to that within man which defiles humanity? Jesus Christ! This is the word of reconciliation. This is the relevance of Christianity.

"God was in Christ, reconciling the world unto himself, not imputing their trespasses unto them" (2 Cor. 6:19). This is the word of reconciliation: forgiveness of sin through the blood of Christ. Sin is the most corrosive influence in life. Who can measure the inefficiency due to guilt?—the breakdown of human machinery caused by guilt? Talk about relevance! Here it is: "God has made Christ to be sin for us, though he knew no sin, that we might be made the righteousness of God in him." God reconciles men unto Himself, "not imputing their trespasses against them." Incredible! This is the word of reconciliation. That is relevance.

Finally, who is to be reconciled to whom? ". . . As though God did beseech you by us: we pray you in Christ's stead, be ye reconciled to God." This is the word of reconciliation: "Be reconciled to God." This is the authentic Christian message—the central thrust of the Church's word to the world: Be reconciled to God!

What is the ministry of reconciliation? "Now then we are ambassadors for Christ." This involves selflessness. We do not represent ourselves, wherever we are, whereever we go; we represent our Lord. Paul says, "We commend not ourselves unto you." We bear His message, His word; there is nothing unilateral in our mission. We are in the world on God's behalf, among those who are alien to God. We are to obey orders from headquarters. We ought to dig into our diplomatic pouch every morning to get our directions. This involves diplomacy, protocol. It has been disturbing to me through the years to observe how difficult it is for some Christians to honor others. They seem congenitally or constitutionally incapable of it. Frequently, this attitude is justified by misunderstanding James when he says that we are not to be a respecter of persons, but Paul commands, "Honor to whom honor is due." I may not like the man, but I honor his office. I may not like the man, but I honor his uniform, the stars he wears as a general. Being an ambassador of Jesus Christ involves protocol. Diplomacy involves courtesy, common courtesy for the sake of Christ. It involves subtlety, "Wise as serpents, harmless as doves."

Being an ambassador for Christ means that we are in the world to represent the best interests of our Lord. But some of us are so undiplomatic, so obvious, so naive, so violent, so arbitrary, so brittle, so inflexible, so self-willed.

[50]

May God give us the softness and the toughness good diplomacy requires.

Being an ambassador of Christ involves tension. We stand between two worlds, two alienated worlds. Often there is militant opposition to Christ's Kingdom. At times we are tempted to withdraw, to lay down arms, to isolate ourselves from this troubled world, to insulate ourselves against its tragedy, to ignore the live issues which keep our world in constant ferment. But these issues will not go away. They are here. They are real. They are facts of life and must be faced in Christ's strength and wisdom.

What is required of us as ambassadors of Christ? Paul reminds us "That he died for all, that they which live should not henceforth live unto themselves, but unto him which died for them, and rose again." This is very plain language. In the light of this requirement it is not difficult to understand the absence of power of the Church in the world. How pathetically self-centered we are. How desperately self-seeking. How defensive of self. How protective of self. How ambitious for self. Think what would happen if every Christian really gave himself away to Christ and began to live, not for himself, but for his Lord, "Who, being in the form of God thought it not robbery to be equal with God: But made himself of no reputation, and took upon him the form of a servant, and was made in the likeness of men: And being found in fashion as a man, he humbled himself, and became obedient unto death, even the death of the cross."

Crossless Christianity is powerless Christianity. Where there is no cross, there is no power. Indeed, where there is no cross, there is no resurrection. Power involves sacrifice. Self-sacrifice. It is so much easier to sacrifice *things* than it is to sacrifice *self*. Today, we are losing out because we struggle so hard to keep what we have and get more—we forfeit all that we hold dear because of our striving to guard it for ourselves. Jesus said, "Whoever shall seek to save his life shall lose it; and whoever shall lose his life for my sake shall find it." Again, He said, "If any man will come after me, let him deny himself, and take up his cross daily, and follow me." This is relevance.

These words are meaningful only as each of us takes it seriously for himself. We do not have to accept this message. We can reject it; that is our prerogative, but we will never be disciples of Christ if we do. We will be a part of the problem in our world, not a part of the answer. But this mission is binding upon everyone of us who professes to be Christian. That is made very clear in the Scriptures. Just imagine, if you can, what would happen if each of us would go as ambassadors for Christ wherever duty calls —living for Christ, not for ourselves, determined in His grace to be a reconciling influence, a redemptive force. Think of it! May God make us this kind of a people.

JESUS AND RACE PREJUDICE

And he said unto them, Ye know how that it is an unlawful thing for a man that is a Jew to keep company, or come unto one of another nation; but God hath showed me that I should not call any man common or unclean.

Therefore came I unto you without gainsaying, as soon as I was sent for: I ask therefore for what intent ye have sent for me?

And Cornelius said, Four days ago I was fasting until this hour; and at the ninth hour I prayed in my house, and, behold, a man stood before me in bright clothing,

And said, Cornelius, thy prayer is heard, and thine alms are had in remembrance in the sight of God.

Send therefore to Joppa, and call hither Simon, whose surname is Peter; he is lodged in the house of one Simon a tanner by the seaside: who, when he cometh, shall speak unto thee.

Immediately therefore I sent to thee; and thou hast well done that thou art come. Now therefore are we all here present before God, to hear all things that are commanded thee of God.

Then Peter opened his mouth, and said, Of a truth I perceive that God is no respecter of persons:

But in every nation he that feareth him, and worketh righteousness, is accepted with him.

Acts 10:28-35

Chapter 5

JESUS AND RACE PREJUDICE

It is impossible to discuss Christian relevance without talking about people. There are two great commandments upon which, we are told by Jesus, "Hang all the law and the prophets." "Thou shalt love the Lord thy God with all thy heart, and with all thy soul, and with all thy mind. This is the first and great commandment. And the second is like unto it, Thou shalt love thy neighbor as thyself" (Matt. 22:37-39). The Apostle Paul wrote: "For this, Thou shalt not commit adultery, Thou shalt not kill, Thou shalt not steal, Thou shalt not bear false witness, Thou shalt not covet; and if there be any other commandment, it is briefly comprehended in this saying, namely, Thou shalt love thy neighbor as thyself. Love worketh no ill to his neighbor; therefore love is the fulfilling of the law" (Rom. 13:9-10). The beloved Apostle John declared in his first epistle, "Everyone that loveth is born of God, and knoweth God. He that loveth not knoweth not God; for God is love . . . If we love one another, God dwelleth in us, and his love is prefected in us" (1 John 4:8, 12). And in his strongest words, "If a man say, I love God, and hateth his brother, he is a liar; for he that loveth not his brother whom he hath seen, how can he love God whom he hath not seen?" (1 John 4:20). Godliness issues in mutual respect and love. No fact is more manifest in the Scriptures. *Christian faith dissolves human prejudice.* Faith that does not do so, whatever its profession, is not just sub-Christian, it is a contradiction.

Peter's experience with Cornelius dramatizes this basic evidence of Christian faith for it represents the surgery of the Spirit on the last vestige of racial prejudice in Peter's heart. Peter said, "You know that it is an unlawful thing for a man that is a Jew to keep company or come unto one of another nation." Never has prejudice been more deeply imbedded in the human heart. History has never known stronger racial prejudice than Peter is talking about here. It is impossible for us today to imagine the contempt with which Jewry held the non-Jew in Peter's day. Juvenal says that the Jews were taught by Moses "Not to show the way except to one who practices our rites, and to guide the circumcised alone to the well which they seek." They would not even give directions to a non-Jew. Tacitus said of the Jews, "Among themselves they are inflexibly faithful and ready with charitable aid, but hate all others as enemies. They keep separate from all strangers in eating, sleeping, and matrimonial connections." Edersheim, in his *Jewish Social Life,* says that "on coming from the market an orthodox Jew was expected to immerse himself to avoid defilement." He might not enter the house of a Gentile, for "He looked upon it to be ceremonially polluted. The Gentile was an abomination. His touch was defiled; his customs were abhorrent; his religion was a blasphemy."

One interesting fact about this is that there is no Old Testament regulation forbidding such social contact. These regulations were added by the rabbis and became binding by social custom. Here is an insight into the human tendency to reduce authentic faith to the traditions of men and to social custom, thereby, in effect, arriving at a Godless religion which has all the form but none of the substance. In the words of Jesus, "Well hath Esaias prophesied of you hypocrites, as it is written, This people honoreth me with their lips, but their heart is far from me. Howbeit in vain do they worship me, teaching for doctrines the commandments of men. For laying aside the commandment of God, ye hold the tradition of men . . . ye reject the commandment of God, that ye may keep your own tradition" (Mark 7:6-9). Peter was committed to this tradition. He said, "It is an unlawful thing for a man that is a Jew to keep company or to come to one of another nation." Hence the possibility of an apartheid policy based upon human tradition which has been elevated to the status of Divine authority. It is not uncommon to hear segregation defended on what is assumed to be Biblical grounds; and thus, to her terrible shame, the Church has been called the most segregated institution in America!

But Peter had come a long way by this time. At Pentecost, he said, "And it shall come to pass in the last days, saith God, I will pour out of my spirit upon all flesh . . . And it shall come to pass, that whosoever shall call on the name of the Lord shall be saved" Acts 2:17, 21). Peter knew of the great spiritual awakening which had

[57]

come to the despised Samaritans through the preaching of Philip. In fact, at the time of this experience he was living in the home of a man whose vocation was held in contempt, but who must have been a brother in Christ, Simon the Tanner, in Joppa. The trade of a tanner was held in such "supreme contempt that if a girl was betrothed to a tanner without knowing he followed that calling, the betrothal was void . . . A tanner had to build his house fifty cubits outside the city." Nevertheless, even though Peter had been baptized with the Holy Spirit, had preached that Pentecostal sermon, knew of the revival in Samaria, and now lived with a tanner, yet an extraordinary act of God was required to break the chains of predjudice in his life.

You recall the story. He was on the house top praying. It was mid-afternoon and he was hungry. He fell into a trance. It was as though "heaven opened, and something descending like a great sheet let down by four corners upon the earth. In it were all kinds of animals and reptiles and birds of the air. And a voice said, "Rise, Peter; kill and eat" (Acts 10:11-13). Now, God had given the Jews very strict rules concerning their eating habits. Obviously they could not eat the food served by non-Jews, but they had projected this beyond food to the non-Jews themselves, and considered them to be unclean. Observe the tremendous and inflexible hold religious tradition can get on a man. Peter responded to the command, "Not so, Lord." Religious tradition can even make a man say "no" to God! Religious tradition, without the love of God, can become the most intolerable influence in life.

Note Peter's self-righteous pride in his reply to the voice: "I have never eaten anything that is common or unclean."

The answer to Peter's obstinance was, "What God hath cleansed that call not thou common." This happened three times, leaving Peter puzzled as to its significance. But he was not left in a quandry for long: "God hath showed me that I should not call any man common or unclean. Of a truth I perceive that God is no respecter of persons, but in every nation he that feareth him and worketh righteousness is accepted with him."

The lesson Peter learned, and which was transmitted to the Apostolic Church, leaves no ambiguity. This is the glorious fact about the true Church of Christ. Here is the thrilling relevance about authentic Christian faith. All races and colors and languages are united in Christ in one inseparable, indivisible bond of love and mission. Paul wrote to the Galatians, "There is neither Jew nor Greek; there is neither bond nor free; there is neither male nor female, for ye are all one in Christ Jesus." And to the Colossians, "There is neither Greek nor Jew, circumcision nor uncircumcision, barbarian, Scythian, bond nor free: but Christ is all, and in all."

This is not just a sociological or humanitarian matter. This is a Christian issue—a decidedly spiritual matter with eternal significance. Peter had to learn, as did his Jewish brethren, that God's redemptive purpose was not exclusive, but universal. It was not nationalistic, but world-wide. It was for all men: "Whosoever shall call upon the name of the Lord . . ." It is fairly obvious that the Apostolic Church learned that lesson. The deplorable tragedy is that the Church in subsequent generations could so easily unlearn, and become as prejudiced and inflexible and obstinate as Peter and his colleagues were in that first generation. Hence the accusation by the world that the Church is irrelevant.

[59]

To many, because of background, culture, traditions, and customs, this may seem harsh and unpalatable. But the Word of God is clear and uncompromising. The issue is critical. It demands a return to the New Testament principle: "God is not a respecter of persons." No man is to be called common or unclean. There are no second class members of the human race. We have committed to us the mission of reconciliation; we have been ordained to be ambassadors for Christ. What an exciting prospect is ours today, when race is such a potent, explosive issue world-wide, to prove the authenticity of our faith by our love for all and our acceptance of all who are acceptable with God. The issue does not center on marches and demonstrations; the real test is our relationship with others personally. This is relevance.

GRACIOUS NEIGHBOR

But he, willing to justify himself, said unto Jesus, And who is my neighbor?

And Jesus answering said, A certain man went down from Jerusalem to Jericho, and fell among thieves, which stripped him of his raiment, and wounded him, and departed, leaving him half dead.

And by chance there came down a certain priest that way: and when he saw him, he passed by on the other side.

And likewise a Levite, when he was at the place, came and looked on him, and passed by on the other side.

But a certain Samaritan, as he journeyed, came where he was: and when he saw him, he had compassion on him,

And went to him, and bound up his wounds, pouring in oil and wine, and set him on his own beast, and brought him to an inn, and took care of him.

And on the morrow when he departed, he took out two pence, and gave them to the host, and said unto him, Take care of him; and whatsoever thou spendest more, when I come again, I will repay thee.

Which now of these three, thinkest thou, was neighbor unto him that fell among the thieves?

And he said, He that showed mercy on him. Then said Jesus unto him, Go, and do thou likewise.

Luke 10:29-37

Chapter 6

GRACIOUS NEIGHBOR

The problem today is not that Christianity is not relevant, but that Christians so frequently give the impression of irrelevance. The Christian gospel has not failed in our presentation—in our demonstration. In reality, the breakdown is at the level of communication—of action.

The role of every Christian is to live and act redemptively in history. As ambassadors of Jesus Christ, we represent Him in a world that is mostly indifferent, uninterested, hostile, but yet in desperate need. Quite understandably, conditioned as it is to the empirical method, our modern pragmatic society insists upon the acid test to any claim or cure—does it work? Demonstration is prerequisite to acceptance. But this attitude is not incompatible with the Christian faith. For example, the apostle Thomas could not accept the fact of the resurrection of Jesus until he had received demonstrable proof. Jesus never ignores the honest demand for proof, and authentic Christian faith has nothing to fear from the most critical demands of honest pragmatism. Indeed, the Master insisted, "If any man is willing to do, he shall know . . ."

It is demonstrable proof in terms of human relationships that can bring reconciliation and healing to a world fragmented by frustrated hopes and unrealized dreams—to a world that is tired of profession but eager to witness the kind of caring that so characterized the relationships of Jesus. Bishop John A. T. Robinson quotes a pioneer contemporary missionary, Horace Simanowski, who labors among the working classes of Western Germany: "Previously the basic problem confronting man was how I can find a gracious God? This question drove men to search desperately for an answer. It was the motor for their action in the world. It unleashed crusades and wars. This cry robbed them of sleep. But we no longer ask this question, or we label it antiquated. But a different question haunts us also. It ignites entire nations. It makes us in our turn victims of anxiety and despair. The question is, how can I find a gracious neighbor? How can we still somehow live in peace with one another?" Bishop Robinson comments: "There lies the difference. The old Reformation revolved around Luther's agonized question and his triumphant, liberating answer, 'by faith alone'. The old Reformation released to men a gracious God, but the world today is not asking 'How can I find a gracious God?' It is asking, 'How can I find a gracious neighbor?' "[1]

This is an exceedingly stimulating thought, and it suggests a fundamental aspect of Christian witness in the world which Jesus vividly dramatized in the familiar story

[1] John A. T. Robinson, *The New Reformation* (London: S. C. M. Press, Ltd., 1965).

[64]

of the Good Samaritan. We certainly know that, generally speaking, our modern world is not lying awake at night looking for a gracious God. But our modern world is certainly languishing for gracious neighbors.

Let's take a fresh look at the Good Samaritan story. It begins: "A certain man"—Jesus deliberately clothed this desperately needy man with anonymity. *It could have been anyone.* Then we see that he had been beaten and robbed and left in the ditch half dead. He was in a desperate condition and needed help. Actually, there was nothing that qualified him for help except his obvious need. And we have no way of knowing whether he was a good man or a bad man. The story doesn't even indicate whether he was religious or not—he just needed help.

Jesus continues the story: "By chance there came down a certain priest that way, and when he saw him he passed by on the other side. And likewise a Levite, when he was at the place, came and looked on him, and passed by on the other side." A casual glance at a suffering man lying helpless in the ditch. Imagine, a priest and a Levite—both pious, religious leaders! Jesus' point is very clear. The very ones who personified the religion of Israel failed completely to communicate the love and mercy and compassion of the God they professed to serve. What a horrible misrepresentation of God, and what a tragic caricature of their holy faith! In reality, they were the epitome of pious irrelevance, and in the words of Jesus they were salt without savor. They may have been good men, but they were good for nothing.

The story continues and the scene changes with the introduction of a new character: "But a certain Samaritan, as he journeyed, came where he was: and when he saw him,

[65]

he had compassion on him, And went to him, and bound up his wounds, pouring in oil and wine, and set him on his own beast, and brought him to an inn, and took care of him." What a contrast! There is no indication that the Samaritan knew the injured man. We have no way of knowing whether the Samaritan was a religious man, but we do know that he was the kind of person who cared deeply about the misfortunes of another person, and that when necessary, he translated that caring into positive and creative action.

The setting for this memorable story is quite significant. Just a few moments before, Jesus had been approached by a young lawyer who inquired as to what he must do to inherit eternal life. Doubtless recognizing that the question was prompted by an improper motive, Jesus parried one question with another. In reply He inquired into his understanding of the law. Apparently without hesitation, the young man responded with a quotation from the ancient Scriptures, "Thou shalt love the Lord thy God with all thy heart, and with all thy soul, and with all thy strength, and with all thy mind; and thy neighbor as thyself." A noble response, but the young man's next question belies the confusion in his own mind: ". . . Who is my neighbor?"

"Who is my neighbor?" This young man wanted Jesus to give him a simple formula outlining precisely whom he should love. Imagine! As far as he was concerned, the burden of proof rested with someone else. It was up to someone else, somewhere, to prove that he deserved the lawyer's love. But Jesus turned the obligation completely around in His parable of the Good Samaritan. He made a point of the fact that this neighbor—the man in the ditch

—was unknown and that it was only his need that qualified him for help. And then at the conclusion of the parable Jesus drove the truth home with penetrating insight when He asked: "Which now of these three, thinkest thou was neighbor unto him that fell among thieves?" Again Jesus ignored the young man's question and asked him another. He made it utterly plain that the burden of proof does not rest upon the one who is supposed to be loved; it rests upon the lover. To Jesus the question, "Who is my neighbor?" was irrelevant—the neighbor was anyone in need, at any place, any time. The young lawyer got the point, and then Jesus made the final thrust, "Go and do thou likewise."

Think of it! All the law and the prophets summed up in two commandments—love God, love your neighbor. The whole moral law of God may be comprehended in these two simple precepts. All that God requires of man may be fulfilled in two uncomplicated duties—love God, love your neighbor. Now, of course, only Jesus fulfilled this moral law, and because of every person's failure generation by generation to love God and love his neighbor, history is filled with woe—mankind suffers indescribable tragedy, the world moves on into ever-increasing and compounded frustration, despite all of its spohisticated, scientific, and technological efforts. To resolve this inexorable process in history, Jesus Christ, the perfect Man, fulfilled the law to perfection, then laid down His life on the cross, suffering the long-term consequences of man's failure and sin, and rose from the dead to bring the transforming power of eternal life to anyone who would receive it by faith.

If this is fulfilling of the law, and Jesus as well as Paul said it is, and if the same Jesus who fulfilled this law now dwells in us who are professed disciples of His, surely there ought to be some evidence of His compassion in us. He was the gracious neighbor. Jesus was the personification of the Good Samaritan in the parable—the Incarnation of love for God and neighbor. However empirical and pragmatic our contemporary world; however indifferent or hostile to Jesus Christ and the gospel; the fact remains that the world in which we live is lost in loneliness and lovelessness. It suffers alienation everywhere. Man is losing his identity. He is Mr. Anonymous—fast becoming a cipher in a meaningless world of computer systems. He languishes for a gracious neighbor.

The Incarnate Christ ascended to the right hand of the Father after He had finished His earthly mission. He had commanded His disciples to wait for Pentecost, fifty days after His crucifixion. Nothing to do but wait. No mission. Wait. Wait for the promise. On that unforgettable day of Pentecost, Jesus Christ sent the Holy Spirit into the world, into history, into the very bodies of believers, to inhabit those bodies, that the Spirit of God might continue the incarnate mission of Christ in us, now indwelt by Him! The true Church is literally the incarnation of Jesus Christ in the world. Surely whatever else we demonstrate to the world, we ought to manifest His love, His compassion.

John begins his Gospel with a so-called prologue. The first words are, "In the beginning was the Word, and the Word was with God and the Word was God." But apparently the Word was not enough, even for God, to communicate with men, because John adds, a few verses later, "And the Word was made flesh and dwelt among us, full of grace and truth." The Word was made flesh. That is evangelical relevance! The world is not listening to our

[68]

words today. It is looking for love incarnate. Words are necessary. The gospel has to be told, heralded, preached, but words are not enough—our lives must literally be the incarnation of what we profess. That is God's way. That is the way of revelance today, and in every age.

THE CHURCH IN THE WORLD

Then came to him the mother of Zebedee's children with her sons, worshiping him, and desiring a certain thing of him.

And he said unto her, What wilt thou? She saith unto him, Grant that these my two sons may sit, the one on thy right hand, and the other on the left, in thy kingdom.

But Jesus answered and said, Ye know not what ye ask. Are ye able to drink of the cup that I shall drink of, and to be baptized with the baptism that I am baptized with? They say unto him, We are able.

And he saith unto them, Ye shall drink indeed of my cup, and be baptized with the baptism that I am baptized with: but to sit on my right hand, and on my left, is not mine to give, but it shall be given to them for whom it is prepared of my Father.

And when the ten heard it, they were moved with indignation against the two brethren.

But Jesus called them unto him, and said, Ye know that the princes of the Gentiles exercise dominion over them, and they that are great exercise authority upon them.

But it shall not be so among you: but whosoever will be great among you, let him be your minister;

And whosoever will be chief among you, let him be your servant:

Even as the Son of man came not to be ministered unto, but to minister, and to give his life a ransom for many.
                              Matthew 20: 20-28

Chapter 7

THE CHURCH IN THE WORLD

One day several years ago I was sitting in a dentist's chair and my good friend, Dr. James Sheets, was working on my teeth. He had just been asked to serve as president of the Inglewood, California school board. Recognizing the fact that such a responsibility would force him to drop much of what he was doing in the church, he asked for my opinion. As he talked, I felt a deep sense of resentment welling up within me. The very idea! What right did that board have to rob "my" church of one of its finest leaders? Fortunately, my mouth was propped wide open and I could not respond immediately to his request for advice. As the moments passed, the Spirit of God began to deal with me, and when I was able to speak, I said something like this: "Jimmie, I can't imagine anything more wonderful than for a committed Christian like you to be president of a board of education in a thriving and growing city."

What a contrast to my previous reaction! When I began

my ministry twenty-three years ago, I planned and labored as though the work of the church consisted in the maintenance and in the prosperity of the establishment . . . and incidentally—my personal success. The work of the church was what we did in the building and for the institution. In short, the work of the church was . . . the PROGRAM. In those days I had one simple criteria for a good member: it was his involvement with the establishment; his attendance at stated meetings; his work for the building and the program. Obviously, a person who attended Sunday school, morning worship, Sunday evening groups, evening service, and mid-week prayer meeting was five times the Christian that someone was who attended only on Sunday morning. I actually resented all competition with community and civic organizations . . . and, above all, other churches. Everything outside "my church," including other Christian organizations, constituted a threat to my success. If P. T. A. met on Wednesday evening, it was understood that prayer meeting would be the choice of the "dedicated" Christian. It was absolutely unthinkable that any good member would let Rotary, or the Chamber of Commerce, or a union meeting, or a school function interfere with his proper "commitment."

What has been the result of this kind of thinking and practice? The church has succeeded in pulling Christians out of the world—out of society—out of community and civic affairs. So often it is a little island of irrelevant piety surrounded by an ocean of need. And our preoccupation with the establishment has been so complete that we have been unable to see the ocean . . . except, of course, if there is someone out there that we want to recruit for the program. The congregation has become an exclusive little system of satellites orbiting around the program . . . or perhaps, it would be more accurate and honest to say, orbiting around the pastor. In the meantime those "secular" institutions out there in the community, lacking leadership which takes God seriously, are so frequently being led by persons who have little or no time for the church. Now we bemoan the fact that labor unions, service clubs, chambers of commerce, school systems, and the government itself have been so thoroughly secularized that the church is on the outside, without influence.

The blasphemous contradiction of this concept began to dawn on me several years ago when I recognized the frustration of good men in the church with nothing to do. For example, Hollywood Presbyterian Church, where I served for nine years, had about 1,750 men on the rolls, but needed not more than 365 to run its affairs. The church I now serve has nearly 300 men and needs only 65 to run the establishment. The sheer absurdity of this caricature of the work of the church comes to light when one sees how busy some pastors are trying to "find jobs" for members . . . and the best they can do is to challenge them to go down to the church on Tuesday evening and paint the chairs in the primary department.

The Church is suffering in the world today because of institutional ego. She is demanding recognition and is falsely preoccupied with her corporate image in society. The ego which is the root of sin in individual man seems to be compounded in collective man. The ego which is such a problem to us as individual Christians tends to be a greater problem to our Christian institutions. And the humility which ought to characterize the Christian should be true of

[75]

his institutions as well. Think of the things that remain un-
finished because somewhere along the line the initiator dis-
covered that he was not getting the recognition he thought
he deserved.

All too often these days the Church is being intimidated
by the wisdom and ways of men—suffering from an in-
feriority complex because she is being told repeatedly
that she has failed contemporary man. If this is true, it is
because the Church has abandoned the message and ministry committed to her by Jesus Christ . . . she is em-
barrassed by her apostolic legacy, and in her lust for relevance has turned to the wisdom of the world in the fight
against sin and evil. She is jumping on the bandwagon of
humanistic movements, thereby failing tragically to be the
unique redemptive force in history that God intended.
There is a basic sense in which the Church, if she is true
to herself, will never receive, and ought not to expect,
recognition from the world. The Head of the Church never
received this recognition. Why should we?

We need to be committed to the ministry of anonymity.
After all, the true influence of the Church cannot be meas-
ured—it is not monolithic or massive. Its true corporate
influence is the aggregate of Spirit-filled, Christ-loving men
and women, gathering for worship, instruction, fellowship,
and prayer . . . then disolving into the society around them
with what William James called "benevolent infection."

The work of the Church is outside the establishment—
outside the church, in the world. And it takes every member to do it! The mandate of the Church is clear: she must
go to the world. All that happens within the church is pre-
paration for work in the world. The measure of what takes
place inside the sanctuary on Sunday is the measure of

what happens from Monday through Saturday, for it is during this period that her members are infiltrating all of the social structures of society. In reality, the work of the ministry—the work of Christ—belongs to the man in the pew, not the man in the pulpit, and it is the holy obligation of every member, wherever he is, whatever he is doing. Every Christian is called of God to be a witness for Christ in every area of life. His vocation is the fulfillment of Christ's mission in the world, irrespective as to how he makes his living.

The false dichotomy of the *sacred* and the *secular* is a devastating hindrance to Christian influence, and we must abandon the spurious notion that the business of the Church is sacred, while the business downtown or in the marketplace is secular; that teaching the Bible is sacred, while teaching in the public school is secular; that worship is sacred, while work is secular. For at least half of Jesus' lifetime He worked as a carpenter, and His public ministry lasted only about three years. Was He involved in *sacred* activities only during that three year period? The answer is painfully obvious! Everything He did was sacred. Even at a very young age He made it clear that He must be "about His Father's business." It is also clear that the Apostle Paul felt strongly about this when he said, "Whatever you do, whether ye eat or drink, do all to the glory of God."

To further illustrate, let me ask two common questions —and I'll supply the conventional answers as they relate to my own church: (1) "Where is your church?" Answer: "5500 River Road, Washington, D. C." (2) "What does your church do?" Answer: "Oh, we're very busy. We really have a program: three services on Sunday, Sunday school for all ages, Sunday evening groups for everyone, midweek prayer meetings, and a very active youth program. We have superb choirs, faithful officers and committees, and active groups for both men and women. We are busy!" So the standard answers go—indicating almost a total preoccupation with the institution.

But, what ought the answers to those questions be? (1) "Where is your church?" Answer: "All over metropolitan Washington, in about three hundred homes and apartments, in schools and clubs, in markets and offices, in the Pentagon, on Capitol Hill—even in the White House." (2) "What does your church do?" Answer: "Many things. She keeps house, teaches school; sells groceries and hardware, clothing and cars, insurance and appliances. She practices law and medicine and dentistry. She makes laws and serves in the military—constructs highways and buildings— serves our government overseas in embassies, in Peace Corps, and in foreign aid programs. Our church is everywhere, in everything, doing everything that needs to be done for the sake of Christ and for the glory of God."

The authentic purpose of the Church is vividly pictured in three simple but very colorful New Testament words: salt, light, servant.

Jesus said, "Ye are the salt of the earth . . ." To be effective and fulfill its purpose salt must completely lose its identity and become a part of what is seasoned—it is of no earthly good as long as it remains in the shaker. But as it is absorbed into the salted object and becomes a part of it, the very character of the object is transformed and takes on the flavor of the salt.

Again, Jesus stated, "Ye are the light of the world . . ."

[78]

Light serves no purpose of itself except to illuminate something else. Actually, we take little notice of the light source unless it is inadequate. When it illuminates properly, we are least aware of it. Normally, we observe and pay attention to what is lighted, not the light itself.

Possibly no incident in the gospel story so colorfully portrays the servant role of the Church as does the account of Jesus washing the disciples's feet following that last Passover supper. Yet, in spite of this classic example of selflessness we are far more inclined to make the gospel serve us—to use it as a protection against the realities of life . . . as though Christ died to preserve the status quo, or to make us more comfortable, or to make the world a better place in which to live.

The extrovert God of John 3:16 does not beget an introvert people. "God so loved . . . that He gave . . ." If this God is in His Church, this love will be clearly seen and demonstrated. And the Church will be compelled by this love to go out to that world in love with the message and ministry of love. This is the work of the Church—the work she has been left in the world to fulfill. Here is the prime example of authentic relevance.

[79]

AS I HAVE, I GIVE

Now Peter and John went up together into the temple at the hour of prayer, being the ninth hour.

And a certain man lame from his mother's womb was carried, whom they laid daily at the gate of the temple which is called Beautiful, to ask alms of them that entered the temple;

Who, seeing Peter and John about to go into the temple, asked an alms.

And Peter, fastening his eyes upon him with John, said, Look on us.

And he gave heed unto them, expecting to receive something of them.

Then Peter said, Silver and gold have I none; but such as I have give I thee: In the name of Jesus Christ of Nazareth rise up and walk.

And he took him by the right hand, and lifted him up: and immediately his feet and ankle bones received strength.

And he leaping up stood, and walked, and entered with them into the temple, walking, and leaping, and praising God.

And all the people saw him walking and praising God:

And they knew that it was he which sat for alms at the Beautiful gate of the temple: and they were filled with wonder and amazement at that which had happened unto him.

Acts 3:1-10

Chapter 8

AS I HAVE, I GIVE

The familiar story of the confrontation of Peter and John with the beggar at the temple gate is highly suggestive and provocative when viewed in parallel with our change-ridden world—a restless world, reaching for utopia. Here is a parable of humanity's helplessness, and her willingness to settle for infinitely less than the best. Here, too, is a lesson for the Church, for Christians to be the redemptive force in history which Christ intended; not to concede to humanity's transient aspirations under the pressure of her lust for the temporal, her indifference to the eternal.

The beggar in this story was totally helpless. Someone had to carry him from his home to his post at the Temple gate. Reduced as he was to immobility, he had one goal in life: "To ask alms." What pathetic resignation is implicit in those three words—his highest hope was to be successful at begging! This is all he expected from life—alms.

On this particular day Peter and John entered the scene. Deeply moved by the physical disability of the pathetic beggar, they paused in front of him. Obviously, such attention provoked even more piteous appeals for alms— something the two disciples did not have. But out of their deep caring—out of their concern for the suffering of another—they gave him healing in the name of Jesus. He didn't get what he asked for, but he got what he needed. He wanted a few coins; he received healing. He had reconciled himself to a life of crawling and begging, dragging his useless limbs in the dust, vegetating. This attitude of apathy is not uncommon in our modern world. Millions of people are resigned to their circumstances and do not even entertain the possibility of serious change in their own lives. Human apathy is one of the most pitiful social tragedies today. How tragic when human nature becomes reconciled to the status quo interminably— human nature reconciled to vegetating; human nature satisfied with a handout.

Incidentally, in spite of the popular criticism of the Church today with reference to some of our ponderous social problems, it has been the Church in history that has moved humanity off the dead center of apathy again and again, and triggered the aspirations for freedom, justice, and dignity in the human heart. It has not been politicians or industrialists; it has been the Church. The Church of Christ through her missionaries brought education, hospitalization, and modern techniques in agriculture to Latin America, Asia, and Africa. Of the first 113 universities founded in the United States of America, 110 were established by Christians who dedicated them to the propagation of the gospel of Jesus Christ and His Kingdom. In fact the revolution in the world today was triggered initially by the missionaries of Jesus Christ, putting into human hearts aspirations that would be satisfied with nothing less than God's eternal answers.

But that is just the point: the danger is that humanity will settle for less than the best—material improvement rather than the healing of the nations, *a sedative instead of a cure.* The temptation is to work with the symptoms rather than with the disease, to try to repair and improve the old decaying order rather than submit to God's perfect order. Humanity is so inclined to settle for a few paltry coins of progress when God wants to give us a shining new world of indescribable righteousness and justice and freedom. It is so easy for the Church, and for Christians, to be enticed or cajoled by sentimentalism or threatened and intimidated by intellectualism, to give the coin of social reform rather than the gospel of the healing and reconciliation through Jesus Christ. We capitulate so easily to the pride of men. We are so easily shamed by high-sounding social or humanitarian ideologies into offering something less than God's redemptive best to mankind. It is so difficult for us to say, "Silver and gold have I none, but such as I have give I unto thee." But we fail when we give *alms* only; we fail God, we fail man, and we fail ourselves.

Because humanity's problem is congenital—sin in the human heart, there is only one solution. This is why Paul could affirm, "I am not ashamed of the gospel of Christ, for it is the power of God unto salvation to everyone that believes; to the Jew first, and also to the Greek." Helmut Thielicke, one of the most effective preachers and authors of the gospel in Germany today, recently published a book

[85]

entitled, *Encounter with Spurgeon.* He recalls that Spurgeon was labeled "the prince of preachers" at a time when preaching had lost its popularity. In spite of the ascendency of modernism, naturalism, and humanism, he preached to 6,000 people every Sunday morning in London, and every Monday morning his entire sermon was cabled to New York City and published in American newspapers. Thielicke writes:

> It was not the aim of his preaching to show people that their life would be easier if they accepted the gospel; that it would solve their problems; that civilization would perish without Christianity; that the State and society need religion; that the Christian social ethic is absolutely indispensable; that the world order needs Christian foundations; that all the misery of modern man comes from secularism; that if our world is to endure there must be a renaissance of the Christian West . . . All this is a kind of high-minded Christian pragmatism which we are all too prone to promote these days, and which frequently enough is smuggled into the Holy City of Ilium under the guise of a Trojan horse called worldly Christianity. All this is completely alien to Spurgeon. He is concerned only with salvation. For us and our kind of Christian social ethic, the threatening danger is that we tend merely to enucleate the Christian ideas concerning the world order, the structuring of society, etc., and then to recommend them for their preservative and productive power. But since it is possible to have the Christian ideas without actually believing, and to be taken up with the social teachings of Christianity, without becoming engaged personally, these ideas lose their connection with the Lord of Christendom and degenerate into ideologies, namely into instrumentalities of power and world mastery. Thus it is possible for Christianity to become merely a pervasive atmosphere, a climate of social order, while faith dwindles away and the matter of salvation is forgotten. Therefore we stand in need of the

[86]

simple way in which Spurgeon dares to say that what really and ultimately counts is to save sinners. Indeed what really counts is that we get to Heaven. Anything else is watered-down social gospel, twaddle—including all the talk about the Christian West.[1]

The head of the Board of Christian Education of one great denomination said recently, "One of our problems is that we have many deliverers of good sermons and few preachers of the gospel." In the final analysis this is what the Church uniquely offers the world, and it is what the world stands ultimately in need of. Let us not sacrifice the gospel for any other message, however relevant and practical it may seem to be, for in so doing we are giving the crippled beggar a coin when we might raise him up to walk and leap and praise God! Dr. Walter Judd on one occasion said that one of the things that troubled him and many of his colleagues in Congress was the fact that preachers and church administrators and Christians in general seem so anxious to get Congress to legislate a kind of righteousness which they are unable to produce in their own congregations. "We can pass laws, but it isn't going to change hearts," said a member of the Senate recently. "We can pass ten million laws, but we'll never change humanity until we find a power that works in the human heart." The conflict, the suspicion, the fear that is strangling mankind in today's electronic age will be dissipated only by the reconciling and healing gospel of Christ.

While Peter and John did not have coins for the beggar, they did have something infinitely better. "Such as I

[1] Helmut Thielicke, *Encounter with Spurgeon* (Philadelphia: Fortress Press, 1963).

have, give I thee," Peter said. You cannot give what you do not have, but you must have, to give. The impotence of many Christians in this exciting, thrilling hour of history is due to the fact that they simply have nothing to offer but a few coins, and alms will not save a sick society. Healing, reconciliation, salvation can be shared only when we have it. We can give only what we have, and some of us are not giving because we do not have.

Not only must you have, to give, you must give, to have. This is not just a play on words, but it is one of the clearest lessons our Lord taught—we cannot keep what we will not give away. So significant is this truth that Jesus phrased it in a variety of ways: "For whosoever will save his life shall lose it: and whosoever will lose his life for my sake shall find it" (Matt. 16:25). In the parable of the talents He said concerning the one who had received one talent and buried it, "Take therefore the talent from him and give it unto him which hath ten talents," because ". . . from him that hath not shall be taken away even that which he hath." Immediately following the giving of the Lord's Prayer in Matthew 6, Jesus gave special emphasis to this truth: "If you do not forgive men their trespasses, neither will your Father forgive your trespasses." That is plain English! He said, "To whom much is given, much shall surely be required." You cannot give what you do not have, and you cannot have what you do not give! I will never forget one of the sayings of Dr. William Evans, great Bible expositor of another generation: "Do you honestly believe that you can get into heaven all alone?" If you have it, you had better share it.

Dr. Luke begins his historical record of the Apostolic Church with these words, "That which Jesus began both to do and preach . . ." He began them; He intends that this Church continue what He began in the power of the same Spirit who enabled Him in His ministry. If we had been with Peter and John on our way to pray in the temple that day, what would we have done? Would we have reached in our pocket, pulled out a few coins, flipped them to the beggar, and walked in pious grandeur into the temple? Or, would we have dared to say, "Silver and gold have I none, but such as I have give I unto you . . ." These are thrilling days to be alive and know Jesus Christ and His gospel. To have it and share it! This is relevance.

CITY OF GOD

By faith Abraham, when he was called to go out into a place which he should after receive for an inheritance, obeyed; and he went out, not knowing whither he went.

By faith he sojourned in the land of promise, as in a strange country, dwelling in tabernacles with Isaac and Jacob, the heirs with him in the same promise:

For he looked for a city which hath foundations, whose builder and maker is God.

Through faith also Sarah herself received strength to conceive seed, and was delivered of a child when she was past age, because she judged him faithful who had promised.

Therefore sprang there even of one, and him as good as dead, so many as the stars of the sky in multitude, and as the sand which is by the seashore innumerable.

These all died in faith, not having received the promises, but having seen them afar off, and were persuaded of them, and embraced them, and confessed that they were strangers and pilgrims on the earth.

For they that say such things declare plainly that they seek a country.

And truly, if they had been mindful of that country from whence they came out, they might have had opportunity to have returned.

But now they desire a better country, that is, a heavenly: wherefore God is not ashamed to be called their God: for he hath prepared for them a city.

Hebrews 11: 8-16

Chapter 9

CITY OF GOD

In the last quarter of the nineteenth century, Marx and Engels gave the world the communist philosophy of history. This divided history into five periods, three of which have passed, the fourth being the capitalistic period, the "'last in which exploitation and class struggle will endure; the period of final revolution, during which all private ownership in the mans of production will be destroyed." Then will come the fifth and final period, when "the only economic changes to be reflected in society would be those leading to ever greater production, ever more leisure for all, and history would, with the dialectic, be transformed into universal tranquillity and peace." This was to take place in three phases: first, violent revolt; second, dictatorship of the proletariat; and third, paradise. Violent revolt against the established order, which is to be followed by a dictatorship of the proletariat, will eventually usher in paradise, a classless society where everybody owns

everything, and all benefits of production accrue to everyone impartially.

Fifty years ago the revolt began, and the communist
world is now managed by the dictatorship of the proletariat
The revolution has a long way to go in many places. Paradise is still as remote as ever where revolt has been successful, and in the Soviet Union at least, infighting among
the proletariat managers has resulted in many modifica-
tions, and in some cases, the adoption of certain capitalistic policies and procedures have been found necessary
to implement the system. Meanwhile, hundreds of thousands, totally committed to this eventual paradise, have
laid down their lives without the slightest participation in
the promised goal; indeed, they never had any hope of the
promised goal.

Despite this failure of communism in its post-revolution-
ary stages to approach its goal, it accuses Christianity of
being an opiate which lures the proletariat to apathy. And
unfortunately, there are many so-called intellectuals in our
western world who have taken this bait, and in so doing
have betrayed their abysmal ignorance of true Biblical,
Christian eschatology. With what futile hope does communism comfort and cannibalize its pitifully blinded and
benumbed disciples, while its leaders piously maintain
control of the "people's property" and enjoy the maximum
benefits of production in the name of the dictatorship of
the proletariat? What greater, more effective opiate to the
downtrodden masses, to the lambs-for-the-slaughter fel-
low travelers, than this classless society of universal tranquillity and peace, to be enjoyed by other generations in
the unforeseen future!

But, some may argue that the comparison is false—

that communism has been at work for less than a century, and that the promise which constitutes the hope of the Church of Jesus Christ was given four thousand years ago to Abraham, and that Jesus Christ, who came to fulfill that promise, died two thousand years ago. Millions have died in the faith of this promise without receiving it; hundreds of thousands have laid down their lives for it; and millions of the faithful have gone to their graves without any personal participation in the promise. Yes, this is true, and this is precisely the point of these words in Hebrews 11: "These all died in faith, not having received the promises."

But at this point the analogy ends, for, unlike the communist hope which promises fulfillment only to future generations sometime, the Christian hope is retroactive. In the words of Hebrews 11:13: "These all died in faith, not having received the promises, but having seen them afar off, and were persuaded of them, and embraced them, and confessed that they were strangers and pilgrims on the earth." The grave is not the end of hope for the Christian, but it is for the communist! Those who died in faith thousands of years ago, embracing this promise, are already with Jesus Christ in glory while awaiting the ultimate establishment of God's eternal Kingdom. This is one thing God is doing in history, He is calling out a people from every nation and language and tribe and color and race and people, generation by generation. He is calling out a people who will live with Him eternally.

I used communism as an example of the futile hope promised by human schemes and systems, but I could have chosen any other of the many social-humanitarian-economic-political panaceas proliferated and propagated by the wisdom and ingenuity of man. From the Tower of Babel to the present moment, every effort of man to solve his problems socially, politically, economically, however cleverly conceived and implemented, has ended in futitity and failure. They are all one hundred percent utopia, which means "no-where." They all fall infinitely short of the glorious, indescribable, universal paradise promised throughout the Bible, which Jesus Himself took seriously and promised to fulfill.

Recently, I had the pleasure of speaking to the residents of one of the homes for the aged in Washington. There were approximately thirty elderly women present, most of them in wheelchairs, all of them very close to the grave. As I looked at their wrinkled faces and worn-out, broken bodies, I realized again how meaningless are all of the eloquent schemes of men for people like this. Communism holds no hope for them, but the Bible does! And then I thought about the maimed and crippled, the broken and the diseased, the victims of tragedy and war. Communism offers no hope to them, but the Bible does! Surely the words of Paul have special meaning for such moments: "I am persuaded that the sufferings of this present time are not worthy to be compared with the glory which shall be revealed in us."

Apparently this is precisely what the faithful people believed and felt whose exploits are mentioned throughout the eleventh chapter of Hebrews. Let's take a closer look at the closing words of that chapter:

> And what shall I more say? for the time would fail me to tell of Gideon, and of Barak, and of Samson, and of Jephthah; of David also, and Samuel, and of the prophets: Who

through faith subdued kingdoms, wrought righteousness, obtained promises, stopped the mouths of lions, Quenched the violence of fire, escaped the edge of the sword, out of weakness were made strong, waxed valiant in fight, turned to flight the armies of the aliens. Women received their dead raised to life again: and others were tortured, not accepting deliverance; that they might obtain a better resurrection: And others had trial of cruel mockings and scourgings, yea, moreover of bonds and imprisonment: They were stoned, they were sawn asunder, were tempted, were slain with the sword: they wandered about in sheepskins and goatskins; being destitute, afflicted, tormented; (Of whom the world was not worthy:) they wandered in deserts, and in mountains, and in dens and caves of the earth. And these all, having obtained a good report through faith, received not the promise.

Why? Because "God having provided some better thing for us, that they should not be made perfect." Commended by God for their faith, the Old Testament saints died without receiving the promises for which they had lived and sacrificed, but they were certain that they personally would enjoy fulfillment one day—that the promise was not just for some future generations.

Abraham is the classic example of this faith. The eleventh chapter of Hebrews defines his faith as follows: "By faith Abraham, when he was called to go out into a place which he should after receive for an inheritance, obeyed; and he went out, not knowing whither he went. By faith he sojourned in the land of promise, as in a strange country, dwelling in tabernacles [that is, tents] with Isaac and Jacob, the heirs with him of the same promise: For he looked for a city which hath foundations, whose builder [architect] and maker is God."

Abraham obeyed. He went out, not knowing where he

was going, and lived in the land of promise as a stranger. He lived in tents because he looked for the city with foundations whose architect is God! Amazing, isn't it, that this nomad, whose home was a tent, and whose possessions were largely farm animals, and whose life was pastoral in the ultimate, should long for a city? What an amazing parallel to our modern world? It seems everybody is moving to the city! In fact the city has become the number one problem of the twentieth century. Apparently there is something in the human heart that causes people to gravitate to the city. In many ways we are critical of cities today and some of us are trying to get away by moving to the suburbs, but we are simply succeeding in creating a megalopolis. Projections insist that our country will be one continuous city from coast to coast and from north to south, along the great arterial highways of the nation. Apparently humanity desires a city, and it shall not be disappointed. We move steadily toward a city—the city of God! The writer of Hebrews is quite explicit that this city, which represents the consummation of Abraham's hope, the consummation of the hope from Adam to the last man who will ever live, was to be conceived and built by God. God is the architect; God is the maker. This is not something man has done, is doing, or will do. It is totally and exclusively the doing of God—not some utopia which is supposed to evolve out of human progress in history. God will do it!

This is authentic faith. It looks beyond the grave. It centers its confidence in an eternal promise. It waits and works and suffers and dies with that eternal promise in view, and this is precisely what the Church needs today. We are not here just to repair this old world and make it as

good as possible. We are here to call men to follow Christ
—to call men out of this world into His Church—to point
men toward "the City which has foundations, whose builder and maker is God." This is our mission! Christians must
outlive, outlove, outsuffer, outsacrifice, outdie the disciples
of any other scheme or program of men. This is Christian
relevance.

POSTSCRIPT

The great difference between present-day Christianity and that of which we read in these letters is that to us it is primarily a performance, to them it was a real experience. We are apt to reduce the Christian religion to a code, or at best a rule of heart and life. To these men it is quite plainly the invasion of their lives by a new quality of life altogether. They do not hesitate to describe this as Christ "living in" them. Mere moral reformation will hardly explain the transformation and the exuberant vitality of these men's lives—even if we could prove a motive for such reformation, and certainly the world around offered little encouragement to the early Christians! We are practically driven to accept their own explanation, which is that their little human lives had, through Christ, been linked up with the very life of God.

There is one other point that should be made before the letters are read. Without going into wearisome historical details, we need to remember that these letters were written, and the lives they indicate were led, against a background of paganism. There were no churches, no Sundays, no books about the Faith. Slavery, sexual immorality, cruelty, callousness to human suffering, and a low standard of public opinion were universal; traveling and communications were chancy and perilous; most people were illiterate. Many Christians today talk about the "difficulties of our times" as though we should have to wait for better ones before the Christian religion can take root. It is heartening to remember that this faith took root and flourished amazingly in conditions that would have killed anything less vital in a matter of weeks. These early Christians were on fire with the conviction that they had become, through Christ, literally sons of God; they were pioneers of a new humanity, founders of a new Kingdom. They still speak to us across the centuries. *Perhaps if we believed what they believed, we might achieve what they achieved.*

(From the introduction to *Letters to Young Churches* by J. B. Phillips)

[102]